AF230871

How To Almost Make It

Mr Fogg

Introduction   7

Be Brilliant   9

Work With The Best   24

Do/Don't Sign With A Major   45

Go Global   58

D.I.Y   76

There's More To Life   95

Never Give Up   104

Lyric References   119

Index   120

Introduction

I have always found rock'n'roll memoirs disappointing. I usually get to the end of them thinking that the author has no more idea of how they became successful than I have. Maybe their success was down to pure luck. Maybe they were just brilliant. Or maybe they are too successful to have to worry about it. By definition we only ever get to hear about the success stories.

I may not have sold millions of records, but I have certainly made plenty of mistakes. And I like to think that I have a pretty good idea of where I've gone wrong – and occasionally right – over the years (you can be the judge of that). My motivation in writing this book is to pass on my learning from the front line of the music industry so that people younger and more talented than me can avoid making the same mistakes.

And, hey, maybe it will also be entertaining.

Be Brilliant

"Keep your teeth sharp and your knives in hands"

We may as well get this out of the way: if you're no good, you're going nowhere. If you thought that I was going to tell you how to be successful with mediocre songs or without practising, I'm afraid I have wasted your time. It may be tempting to conclude from the rubbish you hear on the radio that success is all down to luck, but don't fall into the trap. The thing that makes another artist great isn't always obvious at first glance and, in any case, crossing your fingers and hoping for the best is no kind of strategy. The only way you will be able to look back without regret is to make sure that your music is as brilliant as it possibly can be. It's the one thing within your control.

Perhaps it ought to go without saying, but in my experience the greatest single differentiator between amateur and professional musicians is the amount of time they spend on their music – even if it may not seem like it from the outside. Maybe it's because successful artists are loath to reveal that music is hard work in case it punctures the illusion of glamour. Whatever the reason, you can be reasonably confident that your favourite artist is practising harder and writing more songs than you are.

Now, there may be people out there so talented that they never need to practise or who only ever produce brilliant musical ideas. Assume that you're not one of them. I'm certainly not. My own particular second-rate level of talent has meant that I have had to work harder than most in the pursuit of brilliance. Any small successes I have had have all been the result of pull-out-all-the-stops, up-all-night bloody-mindedness.

****

In 2010, shortly after my first album *Moving Parts* came out, I received an email from the BBC asking me to play at that year's Reading Festival. I had played four years earlier and knew it was a fantastic opportunity, but I also knew from experience that twenty other bands would be in the same position, competing for attention. I was aware that all the performances at the festival were being filmed and decided to make it my aim to put on a show so brilliant that they would be forced to broadcast it. I eventually settled on the idea of having a marching band make a surprise entrance halfway through the set. *Moving Parts* had used marching band sounds on several songs and I thought it would be exciting to be able to see and hear the real thing.

One of the great challenges of creative projects like this is that you just can't be certain that things will turn out how you expect. In my case, I could only afford to have the musicians come for one rehearsal and then do the show itself, which, in theory at least, might be shown on national television. There was no time to experiment; it had to work first time. One of the things that I have had to get good at over the years is working through all the possible risks and obstacles of implementing this kind of idea so that nothing is left to chance. But until it happened for real all I had was the theoretical sound of a marching band in my head.

The first obstacle was finding sousaphone players, which actually turned out to be much easier than expected: I sent a photo of a sousaphone to Andy, the then keyboardist for Mr Fogg, and he replied immediately with two names. I then booked a large concert venue to use as a rehearsal space, cast a majorette from an acting website, gathered together a handful of local percussionists, had a giant MF flag printed and rented a set of marching drums.

I can usually tell in the first ten seconds whether something I have scored is going to work in reality. In this case, it sounded amazing from the first note. The Mr Fogg live show was otherwise at that point heavily electronic and the addition of a live marching band took everything onto another level. I immediately started telling everybody that we were guaranteed to get on TV and – absurdly – we somehow all started to believe that it was bound to happen. Nobody from outside our cocoon had even mentioned the idea, but we had managed to convince ourselves nonetheless. We rehearsed the band's entrance over and over again, and each time they started playing the hair stood up on the back of my neck - even though I happened to be suffering from a severe migraine and could actually barely see what was happening. In many ways the majorette turned out to be the star of the show. She had not only had training in how to properly handle the flag, but also brought her own outfit complete with an amazing, bright blue hat.

On the day of the show itself, everything that possibly could go wrong did, and the whole thing was almost a complete disaster. To start with, the soundcard for one of the two laptops we were using wouldn't send any sound (actually it was just on the wrong setting) so we ended up using the headphone socket, a big no-no. Then, with our line-check already running way past our show time, one of the keyboards started creating a series of weird arpeggios and we couldn't get it to stop. In the end we swapped it with a backup instrument. It wasn't until we were halfway through the first song that we realised that crucial notes on the replacement weren't working, which meant that half the song's bass was missing.

Now, one of the first rules of performance is to ignore mistakes or technical problems and carry on regardless. It may have looked as though I was giving everything to the song, but in my head I was actually performing a series of calculations. By the time we got to the second chorus I had worked out that by sheer coincidence none of the rest of the songs in the set needed the missing bass notes. I was also very aware that we had specified in advance for three of the songs to be recorded for radio; I knew that, however bad the first song may have sounded, all that most people would ever get to hear were those three songs. I was suddenly extremely grateful for the fact that the BBC had specifically advised against choosing the first song of the set for broadcast for technical reasons. I also knew that I had something up my sleeve to win the audience over.

The marching band, waiting behind the stage curtain, had no idea of the technical problems we had been facing and made their entrance with gusto at the agreed moment. The energy it created was incredible. The only downside was that they created so much noise and I got so carried away that I sang the last third of the song totally out of key, but it was a genuinely electric moment.

After the show, everybody was buzzing on adrenaline and had totally forgotten our bold claims about making it onto TV. We had been told by one of the BBC crew that they thought ours was the best performance of the weekend, but thought nothing of it. Then, the following evening, my

Twitter feed started to go crazy. I couldn't work out what it was at first, but then I received a text from a friend saying that Mr Fogg had just been on the primetime TV highlights of Reading Festival. When I watched it back later, I discovered that we had been sandwiched between Arcade Fire and Lost Prophets - both on the main stage - and were the only act from any of the smaller stages to be broadcast. It was surreal to say the least, but felt like vindication for years of hard work and especially the efforts of the previous few days. That week, Radio 1 and 6Music also broadcast songs from our performance.

I was convinced that this was the breakthrough I had been looking for. My manager asked our radio plugger what he could do to exploit it. The answer? He very graciously took all the credit for himself but said, "It's not a game-changer". He flat out refused to speak to any of our radio targets about it. Re-reading his email now, it reminds me just how idiotic and patronising these people can be. You hire them to do a job and they treat you like a child. More of that later, but suffice to say that it was a devastating response from a member of my own team at a time when Mr Fogg was "hot" for once. These opportunities don't come around very often and when they do they last for days if not hours. Not being able to exploit that breakthrough is one of the greatest failures of my career. But the opportunity only arose at all because, for four and half minutes on that day at Reading Festival, we were brilliant.

****

Creating the best music possible sometimes means having to be ruthless. Most of us start out making music with our friends, but not all of our friends are talented musicians and, even if they are, we don't necessarily all share the same taste in music or have the same vision. Some of the greatest bands of all time formed when their members were teenagers, and those bands have a magic that is difficult to replicate. It's far more common, though, to see people being held back by their commitment to talentless, lazy or disruptive band mates.

The bands that I played in in my teenage years consisted of people who were musically able, but whose ambitions were focussed on things beyond music. The result was one person doing everything they could to be as good as possible, write as many songs as possible and get as many gigs as possible, and the others turning up once a fortnight in time for sound check. The band could probably have stumbled on forever, playing the odd gig and generally having a good time, but it would never have produced great music. In the end I had to take the painful decision to split the band up and find people who were more serious - which by the way was harder than I expected. It was unpleasant, but the alternative was giving up the dream of one day making a great album.

The careers of even the most talented musicians can be disrupted by choosing the wrong band mates. I recorded an act not long ago with a singer and drummer whose last band had had two top forty singles, one of which was the title song on one of the biggest movies of 2011. Maybe chart success isn't the most reliable indicator of quality, but the singer is in my estimation an extremely talented songwriter and he and the drummer make a great team. Of the two musicians who make up the rest of the new band, however, one is incapable of discerning between what sounds good and what doesn't but still insists on making their views heard above all others. The result is a long line of failed recordings and unrealised potential. The last I heard, the band was on indefinite hiatus.

I got to see that kind of dysfunction close up when I offered to stand in on bass guitar for a folk band while I was at university. The singer couldn't say no to anybody, and in the end the band grew to be so enormous that it was totally out of control. The group included a "producer" who would make inappropriate noises on samplers during the rehearsals and then be absent at gigs; a power-hungry violinist with diabolical taste; and a kind of mystical presence called "Jamie", who was spoken about with reverence but rarely seen. Jamie was apparently a founding member of the band but had since moved away. It wasn't clear what he did exactly, but the singer Steve believed him to be some kind of genius. The only time I ever met Jamie was at our biggest ever gig at an event sponsored by the city council. It was decided that he should travel to Leeds especially for the occasion to play a children's keyboard. When it came to show time, his main contribution was to smoke a spliff during the performance and have us unceremoniously pulled from the stage by council representatives with clipboards.

Later I recruited a drummer who is now a professional session musician for a new-and-improved version of my high school band. He is and was a fantastic drummer, but one day phoned me up and said he had been offered a better gig and wasn't going to come on a short tour I had flogged my guts out organising. I went and did the gigs on my own and have been a solo artist ever since. Even the best musician isn't worth it if they are going to mess you around.

****

When I was experimenting with the format of my live show in the run up to the release of *Moving Parts*, I thought it would be great to be able to reproduce some of the sampled harp and mallet sounds on the record with a live harpist. The harp is one of my favourite instruments because, apart from looking dramatic on stage, it adds a wonderful sparkle and a real feeling of sumptuousness. After a bit of searching I found a girl called Jem who had been the official harpist of the Prince of Wales, which seemed like a good endorsement if ever there was one. Unlike some classical musicians, she got where I was coming from and immediately understood what was required to integrate the harp into the Mr Fogg live show. I had a performance coming up at a festival in Oxford, so I arranged for the two of us to do the gig along with a trombonist called Faye. It was a great success, and I resolved to try and fit the harp into the rest of my upcoming gigs.

A few days later I received a text from Faye saying something along the lines of, "Your harpist is in Metro on burglary charges. Jokes!" I assumed that this was, indeed, a joke, but discovered to my amazement that she was deadly serious when she brought along a copy of the newspaper to the next show. Apparently "jokes" means "how funny", not "this is a joke" - blame the age gap. Before long, I started seeing Jem in other media, including, eventually, the front page of the Daily Mail. It was alleged that she was a drug addict who had, with her boyfriend, carried out a series of burglaries. The idea of the royal harpist getting involved in this kind of story was a potent combination, and the press couldn't get enough of it. As it turned out, Jem had assumed that I already knew all about it when I approached her, because of all the media attention.

I had booked Jem and Faye for a series of performances in a pop-up Fogg Shop that I was planning for the end of the year. It transpired that Jem's trial was due to take place the week before and, if found guilty, there was a small chance that she might not be granted bail. Jem had told me that she had got caught up in the story through no fault of her own because her boyfriend had used her car to transport stolen goods. I was inclined to believe her and in any case felt that I should support her until the outcome of the trial. Nonetheless, I was in the position of having to wait up until the last minute to find out whether she would be available to play. The call came the night before the shop opened: she had been found not guilty of all charges except handling stolen goods. She was now clean of drugs and I had no doubt that she deserved a second chance.

We spent several days together performing on an almost hourly basis in the Fogg Shop, and I got to know a lot more about Jem's story: she had been in a series of abusive relationships with people who had got her hooked on drugs and was continually being taken advantage of. It was only after she had been going out with the man who had committed the burglaries for some time that she discovered that he had several previous convictions. I felt extremely sorry for her and tried to get her to focus on getting her harp career back up and running, but people in the media continued to hassle her.

The judge had explicitly told her that she should not speak to the press before sentencing, which was due to take place the following week, but she was still being telephoned constantly by journalists and was even being pursued by Max Clifford, who told her that he could make her famous. I tried to persuade her that her best bet was to work hard on her music and be known for that, but her mother was extremely keen that she should partner up with Clifford. His company offered her two months' free PR, during which time he would take the proceeds of any stories he secured. In the end he engineered a two-page tell-all interview in the Mail, which earned him several thousand pounds. Jem got the raw side of the deal: in return for filling Max Clifford's pockets she was forced to reveal details of drug taking in royal palaces.

As long as Jem continued to do a good job for Mr Fogg, however, I continued to support her. But after a while she started to become sloppy. After a session for Q Radio in which she made mistakes that indicated she hadn't been keeping up with the music, I felt I could no longer risk the damage to Mr Fogg. It was very sad to let her go, especially as I felt that Mr Fogg had been one of the few constants during a difficult period. I hope that since then Jem has managed to shrug off her tabloid reputation and put her focus back onto music.

Work With The Best

One of the rarest things in the world is talent. There are thousands if not millions of people who can perform a convincing impression of their favourite singer or paint a passable watercolour of a rural landscape. True brilliance is much harder to find. For those of us trying to make our way in the creative industries that means that we have to choose our partners wisely. It's easy to find an art or film school graduate with the skills to do an average job and actually if you've got the money it's relatively easy to find people who are both talented and successful. The challenge for most of us is being able to identify really talented people that we can afford. I've always gone out of my way to try and work with the best possible people. Believe me, cutting corners on the quality of your collaborators is no way to get good results.

In late 2009 I was on the lookout for somebody to direct the video for *Moving Parts*, which was going to be the first proper single from my debut album.

I had read dozens of pitches from up-and-coming directors but wasn't really excited by any of them. For inspiration I decided to edit some movie footage to one of my songs and ended up using the beautifully shot black and white sequences from the film *American History X*. The combination of the music and those images was a million times more powerful than any of the ideas that were being pitched to me, so I immediately resolved to try and get in touch with whoever it was who had created them. It turned out that the director and cinematographer was a filmmaker called Tony Kaye.

Tony is the archetypal flawed genius. He is the most decorated director of television commercials of all time, a two-time Grammy-winning maker of music videos and the director of an academy award-nominated feature film. And yet his output post-X consists of a documentary about abortion that was shortlisted for an Oscar but took 18 years to make, a thriller starring Laurence Fishburne that was never finished and an indie movie called *Detachment*, which featured Adrien Brody and Brian Cranstone but went largely unseen. In hindsight it's the phrase "18 years" that should have rung alarm bells.

In my innocence (and ambition – my first album had yet to come out and there was still a very small chance that I was going to be a pop star) I tracked Tony down on Facebook and sent him a grovelling message asking if he would be interested in discussing making a music video for Mr Fogg. If the fact that it had taken him 18 years to finish *Lake of Fire* hadn't got my attention, his email response certainly did.

Let's talk
Make angels
Run from praise
Shrink time
Crave fear
Tony
!

For all I knew this was how all Hollywood film directors talked. I certainly wasn't put off. Intrigued, yes. Worried, not really. But it was definitely weird enough to get me doing some more research. It turns out that Tony Kaye is the protagonist in one of the best-known and strangest Hollywood stories around.

Having moved to LA after a successful career in commercials, Tony got his big break with *American History X*, which was funded by New Line Cinema. But he started to get agitated by how the studio and Ed Norton – the movie's star - were influencing the edit. He managed to buy himself eight weeks to turn in a director's cut, but only after booking full-page adverts in *Daily Variety* and *The Hollywood Reporter* slating Norton and New Line. In the aftermath he brought a rabbi, a priest and a Tibetan monk to a meeting with the studio; tried to have his credit on the movie changed to Humpty Dumpty; and finally earned himself a place on the Hollywood blacklist when he turned up dressed as Osama Bin Laden to direct a film shoot starring Marlon Brando.

When I eventually met Tony, however, I have to confess I found him perfectly reasonable. We talked about a film he was making for the Copenhagen climate change conference over a couple of soft drinks and agreed to try to work together. I remember thinking back to that black and white footage from *American History X* and saying to myself that if I could just keep him on track I was confident he would produce something brilliant. I had no idea how difficult a task that would be.

Over the next few weeks Tony and I batted ideas for the video back and forth over email. He continued to write in his unique style but enthused about the project. When I told him that I was performing eight times a day in a pop-up Mr Fogg shop in London, his reply was typically over the top.

That is genius man
Absolute genius
Absolute genius
Absolute genius
8 is a great number
You cannot fail
Keep making angels

At this point I probably should have realised that not everything he said should be taken at face value, but I was much too excited to be working with a Hollywood director and booked my flights to Los Angeles for the shoot.

The first sign of trouble ahead was when Tony stopped responding to my emails. I was arriving in LA in a few days' time and I couldn't get a squeak out of him. All the grand plans he had described had apparently dissolved into thin air. I couldn't even get him to give me an address to put on my visa. Eventually, two days before I was due to fly out, he sent me a message saying he would pick me up at the airport and that he had a plan that was "loose, but valid".

The loose-but-valid plan turned out to involve sweet-talking staff at various iconic theatres in LA into letting us take pictures. They thought we were taking the photos to scout for a film location, but Tony actually planned to animate the photographs into the video itself, thereby getting the locations for free. It was quite something to see him at work. At one point he talked his way into the Frank Gehry-designed Disney Hall and managed to persuade the manager to let me play its legendary pipe organ, considered one of the finest musical instruments in the world. Later our tour guide took us up into the lighting gallery and Tony lay on the glass floor and asked me to take a photo of him pretending to fall through the ceiling. Quite apart from the powers of persuasion, though, Tony's photography was spectacular. He would regularly point his camera at an apparently unremarkable street corner or section of seating and something otherworldly would come up in the viewfinder.

In fact the three days that we spent shooting couldn't have been more fun. We were driven around in one of those enormous black LA cars you see on TV except Tony's was full of half-finished art canvasses and musical instruments. He told me that he would like to show me the recording studio in his house (apparently all the interior walls have been taken out so it looks like a big white exhibition space) but he had lost the key and hadn't been able to get in for weeks. Tony was obsessed with *Avatar* at the time ("It's crap, I mean fucking crap but, you know, fucking amazing") so we even filmed some performances in 3D. The week ended with a shoot in downtown LA at the ungodly hour of five in the morning and then I flew to New York to do a TV show (which was never aired by the way – another great success) thinking that I had done it. I'd actually got Tony Kaye to direct a music video for me.

The problem was that the shoot itself wasn't even half the job. Tony had three thousand photographs to edit, not to mention a day's worth of green screen footage. To start with, though, the updates were positive.

It is going amazing
This is going to be way better than I even thought
Nothing, absolutely nothing will be diminished
Freedom

But Tony's emails started to dry up. I began to wonder how much work he had actually done. Before I knew it we were in May and the release date for the single had come and gone. Tony hadn't delivered so much as a rough cut. I managed to arrange a premiere during the Cannes film festival to try and regain momentum, but Tony failed to deliver an edit even for that despite promising to do so.

At this point Tony pulled what I now understand to be the ultimate diversionary tactic and asked me to write the score for a movie he had been asked to direct starring Adrien Brody. Frankly, I knew even then that the chances of a note of my music ending up in that movie were less than thirty per cent, but it was simply too great an opportunity to ignore. I see now that for Tony it was just another reason for me not to scream at him down the phone. Nonetheless, I pursued the outside chance of writing that score like a dog chasing a tennis ball. After a lot of persistence I eventually discovered that Tony was coming to London for the edit. I gave him one hour's notice and turned up at the edit suite.

I walked in to find a typical scene of Tony Kaye chaos. He had grown an enormous beard and was sitting in the corner of the room surrounded by the contents of an open suitcase. He greeted me like an old friend, saying, "You have played this *absolutely* brilliantly". I'm still not entirely sure what he meant, but I can't say I agreed. I had hired somebody to make a music video for a song that had now been released 7 months ago and – although I had only paid a third of his fee up front - wasted a lot of money in the process. But Tony was as charming as ever: he had people working on the video even as we spoke but also wanted to be sure that I was willing to write some music for his movie; he would have a rough cut for me on DVD in 24 hours to look at for score ideas. Should

I have believed him? Certainly the situation was getting more and more preposterous, but a DVD in the post on Tuesday still seems somewhat concrete to me even now. In practice, it was pure fantasy.

My last-ditch attempt at breaking Tony's inertia was to send him a testy email almost exactly a year after the original shoot. His response was perhaps the most ridiculous of all his communications: "Happy Anniversary [sorry]". But, almost unbelievably, in the same email was a link to a video website. The link was password protected and it took Tony a full two months to come up with the password, but in March 2011 I finally found myself watching three minutes of animated photography, some of it indifferent but some of it wonderful. Spurred on yet again on the wild good chase I tried to persuade Tony to finish it and he agreed. Then, radio silence.

Two months later, mournfully watching the half-finished video that Tony had sent me, I noticed that it had been posted not by Tony himself but on somebody else's profile. Through a bit of Internet stalking I discovered that that person was an animator called Ana based in Los Angeles. I eventually managed to set up a Skype call with her and learned that Tony had arrived at Ana's studio with a suitcase full of photos in early 2010, told her to "make monsters" and never come back. Tony had never paid her for the animation she had uploaded and she hadn't heard from him in months. It felt like the project was dead in the water, but Ana and I were at least united in our frustration. In the end I paid her a nominal $500 to complete another round of animation and cut the resulting footage into something resembling a music video. The version that was eventually released a year after it should have been is my edit of Anna's animations of Tony's photos.

What we ended up with is nowhere near what Tony and I could have achieved if he had just put his mind to it, but I don't regret taking the risk. I had a chance to work with a genius and I took it knowing the outcome was uncertain. The potential for greatness made it seem worthwhile even up to the last moment. Tony's film with Adrien Brody – *Detachment* – was eventually released in 2012. My music got nowhere near it, but still part of me couldn't resist cheering along with Tony for getting his first feature made since *American History X*. I went to watch it in at an empty cinema in Soho one afternoon. It was flawed, but compelling – like Tony himself. My last contact with Tony was two years later. I dropped him a line to say I was in LA for a few days. He replied to say he was away in London. Typical.

****

My musical collaborations have generally been less catastrophic, but it did take me a long time to find the right match in a record producer. The first Mr Fogg recordings were done in my parents' spare bedroom – a cliché if ever there was one – and had somehow got played on the radio despite all their technical limitations. But when the time came to get serious I knew I needed to work with somebody who could make my songs sound as good as my heroes'.

I had read an article in the local paper about a record producer living nearby who had been successful in the 70s and 80s, so turned up to bug him at a concert the article said he was organising. The producer turned out to be Martin Rushent, who was most famous for his work with the Human League but also produced The Buzzcocks and The Stranglers and even engineered *Get In On* by T-Rex. Nothing really came of our conversation, but then a manager called Harry Barter bumped into him in the local supermarket and they ended up talking about a demo I had sent to each of them. They both happened to be looking for a project to work on and they agreed that that project should be me.

My first meeting with Martin was – as I learned later - pretty typical. I met him at a pub called the Red Lion, which I soon learned was his home from home, and discovered that he had actually arranged to meet somebody else for lunch at the same time – Martin was always inviting incongruous combinations of people to the same meeting without warning any of them. Martin's lunch guest was a woman in her sixties who dressed and acted like a cross between a star from the golden age of Hollywood and an ageing drag artist. She fawned over Martin like he was a demi-god (actually, maybe that's why Martin had arranged for her to be there) and talked at length in a manufactured voice about her plans for his autobiography. We had a brief discussion about music during which it turned out that Martin had never actually got around to listening to my demo and then we went back to his house to see his studio. In practice this meant me sitting stiffly in the lounge while he and his guest went to smoke a joint in the back. Eventually Martin came back in to tell me that he was moving house and I would have to help him rebuild the studio before we could record. A fair enough deal – he wouldn't be paid for the recording sessions unless they were a success.

Martin told me that the studio should only take a week to complete, but I ended up spending the best part of the next year in and out of his house. For most of the summer of 2006 I crawled under desks, carried speakers, fitted coloured lights and organised and re-organised boxes of cables and fittings. We still hadn't recorded a note of music, but I was learning a huge amount. Most home studios nowadays consist of a computer, a microphone and maybe the odd compressor or pre-amp, but Martin had filled a spare bedroom with wall-to-wall patch bays, racks of flashing equipment and a mass of musical instruments. And the technology went far beyond anything useful. He had gone to great lengths to perfect his setup for listening to *The Archers* on BBC Radio 4 and built a custom fader switch for the multi-coloured mood lighting we installed. All of this seemed to require endless trips to Maplin on my part and of course plenty of cups of tea. There is a great tradition of studio assistants making tea for producers (how I became the assistant I'm not quite sure – I thought I was the artist!) and in Martin's case it was two teabags per cup, milk up to a pre-designated line and squeezing the bags vigorously to get out the "strongest liquor".

After a while I seemed to become part of whatever was going on around the house. I regularly used to pick up Martin's daughter from school and remember especially vividly almost falling off a ladder trying to attach a giant snowball to a tree in the garden for his birthday party. Once the studio was up and running the same applied to Martin's musical projects, which ranged from the sublime to the ridiculous. Martin's name was constantly being exploited by a long line of local village "talents" who – like me – came to him expecting him to turn them into stars. A memorable low was recording fifty-two takes of a pitchy Anastasia tribute singer that even after a full day's editing didn't amount to a presentable performance. On another occasion I was tasked with translating a song by "the French Craig David" into English (for which I'm still owed three hundred quid). But Martin was also involved in some more interesting things, one of which was the beat boxer Killa Kela.

Kela had just been dropped by BMG and was trying to get some material together to pitch for a new deal. After the end of the first day we had written a song and recorded half of the vocal. It had been recorded after a drink or two and was technically all over the place, but had a definite vibe to it. The problem was that when Kela came back sober the following week he couldn't get the second verse to match. So we all had to pile down to the Red Lion to resolve the issue. Apparently the pub's lager wasn't doing the trick so I drove them down to the local off-license where Kela, in moon boots and sunglasses, asked a polite middle-aged man in a sweater if he'd "Got any Veuve, mate?" By the time we got back to the house Martin was roaring drunk and blasting The Who *Live at Leeds* down the street. Still, the track got finished.

As far as my own music was concerned, working with Martin was a revelation. His mixes sounded enormous and my voice was unrecognisable from my demos. I made sure I took in as much as I possibly could: a touch of EQ on the kick drum at 1k, synth lines doubled in different octaves, keyboards turned into orchestral arrangements and a surprising amount of treble on the bass guitar. He also taught me how to compile even the most hopeless vocal takes into the perfect edit, the magic tuning effects of a doubled voice and the power of mix bus compression. When Harry Barter came over to hear the results he rolled up his sleeves to show us the hair on his arms standing on end. We'd made a hit, several in fact if you asked Harry.

We put out Martin's version of *Stung* as a 7-inch, but eventually I came to realise that as epic as Martin's mixes were they sounded like they came from another era. Neither Harry nor Martin could hear it, but I knew that the recordings sounded out-dated. For all of his talent, Martin had just been out of the limelight for too long.

Tragically, Martin passed away in 2011 aged just 62. He had made fits and starts of progress towards making new records but was ultimately too stubborn and chaotic to compete with the new generation of producers. His family and friends organised a private music festival to commemorate his life. He would have loved it. The highlight was Kela absolutely smashing it in front of a crowd of bemused villagers. Actually Martin did start work on that autobiography but it fell by the wayside like a hundred other projects. I hope it eventually sees the light of day so that more people can hear his stories about being hit over the head with a mic stand by Shirley Bassey, accidentally destroying the final mix of *War of The Worlds* and being chased down the street by Jerry Lee Lewis.

****

After several other experiments I eventually came to meet Valgeir Sigurðsson, who is probably still best known for working with Björk on *Vespertine*, *Drawing Restraint 9* and *Medulla*. I think we must be the least effusive creative partnership ever forged. When I first met him at a show in Brighton he couldn't have seemed less excited by the prospect of working with me. It was a bit like one of those "brush-by" meetings that British politicians try to organise with American presidents. But, instead of Gordon Brown attempting to have a meaningful conversation with Obama in a kitchen, I was parachuted in 5 minutes before stage time for an awkward chat about bassoons. As it turned out, that may be the secret to our working relationship: not a lot of talking, plenty of getting stuff done. Valgeir once joked that I should include a Mr Fogg excite-o-meter with the album artwork to correspond to my measured responses to his mixes – "fine"; "good"; "ok".

One of the most unpleasant things for a songwriter is having other people suggest terrible ideas. Actually they may not be terrible ideas at all, some of them might even be brilliant, but if something doesn't fit with your vision for the song it jars like nothing else. It's like having somebody try to reach inside your skull and manipulate your brain. Working with record producers for me has often consisted of them suggesting a series of "terrible" ideas and me vetoing them until there's nothing of value left for them to add. Somehow Valgeir has always managed to suggest things that I find tasteful, and I suppose I've become better at letting in good ideas over the years.

He is also extremely willing to break the unwritten rules of mixing. The first song I recorded with

Valgeir featured both a massive distorted bass guitar part and a heavy synth bass. Just the previous week I had recorded the same song with another producer who had insisted that it wasn't possible to include both parts. Valgeir simply panned the bass guitar hard to the right and turned it up good and loud. Problem solved.

When I got back from that trip I put the two songs we had recorded together on the car stereo on the way back from the airport and immediately felt tears streaming down my cheeks. For the last three years I had travelled from one studio to the next in search of the sound in my head and each time the finished mix came up on the big speakers it had seemed close, but the recordings all sounded weak when I got them home. It was an amazing feeling to know that I had finally nailed it and that I knew how to do it all over again for the rest of the album. Those two songs were *A Second Look* and *Moving Parts* – they ended up being the first two tracks on my debut album.

Since then Valgeir and I have co-produced two studio albums. When I decided to go it alone for the third and discovered there was a song – *Time To Ascend* – that I couldn't get right, I sent it to him to mix and he nailed that too. I'm just a footnote in his career – he has since worked with Damon Albarn and Feist as well as his brilliant Bedroom Community collaborators – but he is a big part of mine.

Any artist worth their salt has strong views about how they want things to sound, but I have come to learn over the years that if you give the right person a chance to come into your bubble you can create things even beyond what you thought was the ultimate vision. It's absolutely crucial to give yourself the chance to take advantage of other people's input, but also that you are working with the right person - working with the wrong people can be equally damaging. For me, that also means that ignorance is never an excuse. Too many artists are over-reliant on co-writers or producers because they have never developed the skills themselves to be able fight their corner. So: know your own mind, know what you're talking about, but give yourself the chance to benefit from collaboration. And work with the best.

Do/Don't Sign With A Major

"I've got the key if you want it – I've got your throat in my hands"

Much of the debate around the performance of major record companies is carried on by outsiders with an axe to grind. This is no exception. I have had many run-ins with major record and publishing companies over the years, but none of them is yet to offer me a multi-million pound advance, so you should perhaps bear this in mind when reading my apparently balanced analysis.

I have been the next big thing (or one of them) somewhere between two and three times. The first time, in 2006, I had just managed to get my demo played on three of the country's four biggest music stations, received an offer to release a 7-inch single from an independent record label and been booked to play Reading Festival, all without so much as a manager, plugger or booking agent. My music stood out a mile from all the 4-piece guitar bands that had followed The White Stripes and The Strokes over the cliff in the early 2000s, and the prospect of combining that early potential with serious resources was exciting.

Knowing very little about the music business I made perhaps my first major career error by joining forces with Harry Barter. Harry got my attention because he had an enormous house full of gold discs and because he was the first person in the music industry to show any interest in me. I actually still believe that he might have made a success of Mr Fogg if he had really put his mind to it: he was steely, persuasive and genuinely believed in the songs. Unfortunately, it soon became clear that his rather less talented son would be doing most of the legwork, as Harry was semi-retired. For a while, though, it looked like things were going pretty well. Harry found a radio plugger who did a great job on Radio 2 and 6Music, and before long I was receiving emails from A&R people at all the major record companies.

The meetings we had with those people were interesting to say the least. A junior scout at EMI called Phil Christie, who is now head of A&R for Warner Brothers Records, insisted that my music should be more Keane-like and offered to pay for a recording session with a producer who was best known for working with Kylie Minogue and whose Myspace page said he was a scientologist. After each meeting, Barter junior would say, "By the way, *you* wouldn't be able to tell, but that went really well" in a way that implied that he and A&Rs spoke a secret language that I would never understand. I didn't reveal that I had spent much of my time at university wearing a t-shirt with "Save Music: Destroy Travis" on it and that in my mind Keane were basically Travis-lite. Instead I duly arranged to travel down to Hastings for the session. It was cancelled at 12 hours' notice because the producer had been called in urgently to make a new record for Jamelia after her third album had disappeared without trace. I never got to find out whether he really was a scientologist.

The second EMI-sponsored attempt at a hit record was conducted at the publisher Peer Music's studio, which was offered for free as part of an ongoing courtship. The producer was Howie B, who had previously worked with Björk and U2. Phil Christie sent me a personal message the night before saying how excited he was to hear the results.

On the first day of recording, Howie told me that I shouldn't worry about the production and should instead focus on my vocals. He and his assistant would create all the music. He had brought a vintage drum machine with him and proceeded to program a completely inappropriate beat without listening to the song first. In the hope that Howie knew what he was doing and that it would come good in the end, I allowed him to dictate play for the first day. But the track only became further removed from what I had intended. On the second morning, with the feeling that the whole episode was turning into a slow motion car crash, I went in early and reprogrammed the drums before Howie and his assistant arrived. I think he was surprised that I even knew how it was done. But the gap in vision was just too great; what we ended up with was more Howie B than Mr Fogg. It's nobody's fault really, just a musical mismatch - the sort of thing that happens all the time and you put down to experience. Unfortunately, EMI, Peer and my lawyer were all due to come and listen to the finished record at 6pm that day, expecting to hear a smash hit. What they actually heard was a kind of garagey dance remix, and they were extremely unimpressed. The next time I spoke to Phil he said he had no idea why we were even bothering to try and work with Howie B - he was a "vibes man" who had got lucky and there was no way it was ever going to work. Quite a change of tune.

Despite this obstacle, we stumbled on and eventually came up with a Martin Rushent-produced version of the song that everybody was happy with. EMI agreed to fund its release, and Peer told us (or at least the Barters told me) that we would also receive a deal offer from them within 48 hours.

We heard through our lawyer that EMI were working on a contract that as well as the single would also include options for several albums. Instead of trying to negotiate for more resources or different terms, or even actually reading the offer, the Barters told EMI (without consulting me) that we couldn't agree to such a deal. I think they felt that as we had many other interested parties they could just go elsewhere and get a better offer, but there was also a definite flavour of bravado about the whole thing. Since we never did see anything in writing, maybe it was the right decision, but in any case another offer never materialised. Instead EMI gave us some money for radio promotion but became increasingly detached. Around the same time, while I was busy in the studio one day, the Barters went out for lunch with Peer's US and UK heads of A&R and apparently managed to mess things up sufficiently that we pretty much never heard from them again.

The Barters and I eventually fell out after I asked Barter Jr. to confirm that the 7-inch records for the *Stung* single had been pressed by the label in time to be distributed to retail. He said they had, only to come to me two weeks later in a panic because the label hadn't manufactured any product at all and we were going to miss the release date. Harry and I had a pretty impressive swearing contest the following week, and I decided not to renew their contract. It was only then that all the people the Barters had been speaking to on my behalf came out of the woodwork to tell me how little confidence they had in them.

Reflecting on that period, though, it's hard for me to claim too much artistic high ground in setting up my own label to release my music. As far as I knew the route to success was with a major, and if an offer had come along I likely would have taken it - I've turned down countless offers from both labels and publishing companies in the subsequent years but nothing on that scale. But it's also clear to me that at least part of the reason why I didn't end up signing to a major at that time was that I refused to play ball. I knew that Keane was the wrong marker for my music - I was more interested in Björk or Radiohead, who sell millions of records but still aren't considered mainstream influences by A&R people - and I disagreed fundamentally with the production and marketing ideas that were put to me.

I also find it hard to attach too much regret to that period. While I have gone on to make three albums with total artistic control and absolute certainty that they will be heard, many of my friends and contemporaries have made records that will never see the light of day. The big downside is the possibility that having total artistic control has led me down a path of a certain level of commercial obscurity. But the stories of friends and colleagues like The Good Natured, Goldrush, My Luminaries, Pure Reason Revolution, Morning Runner and many others - bands that most people will never hear of - make it clear that signing to a major label is no guarantee of fame and fortune either. In any case, I want to make music that sends a shiver down my spine, and that's difficult to do to order.

****

It is from this viewpoint that I approached my second period as a next big thing in the first half of 2012. I had released my first album in 2010 and almost succeeded in cracking the media: my performance at that year's Reading Festival was broadcast on primetime television, my self-directed video for *Answerphone* had reached over 100,000 views and the record had been supported by Radio 1, Radio 2, NME, The Guardian, Q Magazine and pretty much every other major music publication in one form or another. But by the time I came to release my second album - *Eleven* - I was considerably more cynical and pessimistic about my chances of doing the same (or better) again. I had been through the wringer once already and was distinctly disillusioned by how little impact all that activity had made on my career. To my amazement, however, the first single - *Stay Out Of The Sun* - was played by Zane Lowe as "Next Hype" on Radio 1. Zane Lowe is perhaps the most influential DJ in UK music radio and I had tried and failed to persuade him to play at least five previous singles. By giving me the "Next Hype" endorsement, he was indicating that I was one of the acts to watch that year.

That week I received a stream of emails from managers, labels and publishers. It was like 2007 all over again, but this time I took none of them at face value. When they made amorous noises I was appreciative but not over-excited; when they told me that their legal teams were working on deal proposals I expected nothing. I played a straight bat, went to all the meetings, took all the calls, but absolutely refused to put everything on hold for them. By the end of March I was having serious next-stage conversations with 12 different publishers, record companies or managers. At least four or five of them told me I should expect to receive a deal proposal.

In April the album came out accompanied by a second single. Zane didn't play it. The phone stopped ringing.

If you haven't experienced the lore of the music business, it's hard to believe that an industry could be so gutless as to outsource all its decision making to one radio DJ, but that's certainly the impression with which I left the experience. And it's a sobering lesson for all those artists who aren't in control of their own careers. If I had been on a big label I would have been dropped in an instant. As it is, the record was released and enjoyed by thousands of people around the world (albeit not enough to revive the profits of Universal or Sony).

****

At the end of 2013 I took a year out from music to study for an MBA at Oxford University. I was frustrated with the punch-drunk state of the record industry and felt that if I wanted to be able to tackle its ills I would first need some formal business skills. The first chance I had to put this theory into practice came the following summer, when I had the opportunity to do some consultancy work for Radiohead's management. One of the projects I worked on was the release of Thom Yorke's album *Tomorrow's Modern Boxes* through BitTorrent. That experience really rammed home for me where it is that major labels are letting the side down. For all the analysis I threw at them, Radiohead's team had one belief above all: if the music is great, the finances will take care of themselves. It's a simple idea, but it requires more bravery than you might think. Many great music fans work in major record companies and their A&R teams can tell you the name of every upcoming act and every genre or style that happens to be waxing or waning at a given moment. But the challenge is, in the face of musical trends, media analysis and social media statistics, to be able to say with confidence that you believe in a piece of music, and give it the chance to reach an audience.

The other way in which Radiohead buck the trend is their use of digital technology. Ever since Kazaa and Limewire, the major record companies have been too terrified and too bound by complicated licensing frameworks to fully embrace the possibilities of digital distribution, which are surely far more diverse than iTunes and Spotify. A major record label would never have tried pay-what-you-want as Radiohead did with such success for *In Rainbows*. A major label would never have experimented with BitTorrent in the way that Thom Yorke has. They simply have too much to lose. For us artists, the question is therefore whether major labels have the flexibility to create the best opportunities in today's diverse digital landscape.

Maybe all of the above leaves you wondering why the word "do" is in the title of this chapter. Well, the simple fact is that the vast majority of the most successful records are still released on major labels. Even independent-minded artists like Arcade Fire and Macklemore still rely on the marketing and distribution of the majors. Even for Radiohead it was a major label that funded the touring and promotion that built their fan base early in their career. It may be easier and cheaper than ever to record a song and distribute it around the world, but the sheer quantity of music in today's marketplace means that the odds of reaching a mainstream audience are longer than ever. Not all music should have that aim, but some demands and deserves it. Many people believe that in the digital age it is enough to make brilliant music and wait for the audience to come to you. My view is that it takes a certain amount of resource to cut through the noise.

For those of us closer to the bottom of the ladder there's something else worth considering. One saving grace of the major is the fact that they pay an advance up front and take the risk on being able to turn the act into a profitable business. For a band living out of a van that can sometimes mean the difference between carrying on and having to give up. So I'm slightly more sympathetic to bands that "sell out" than you might expect.

Whichever way you release your music, you can't avoid risk. Signing with a record company involves the possibility that your blood, sweat and tears may never see the light of day; going it alone carries serious financial risk. Both can kill your career. For that reason, I don't think there is a single right answer to how an artist should release their music in 2015. The good news is that there is now an option to suit every kind of artistic and commercial aim.

Go Global

"Why not take a chance – Sprint"

When I started playing in bands in Reading in the mid 90s, the generally accepted route to success was to rise to the top of the bill at Bar Oz - a subterranean bar opposite the railway station accessed through what looked like a public convenience - and then to play a gig for a "big London promoter" at a pub in Camden, where you would be spotted by somebody from a major record company and catapulted to fame and fortune. Bands implemented this strategy with verve and came back with wild tales of men with record bags who handed out business cards at The Dublin Castle or The Bull and Gate. Everyone referred to these acts as the "Big Reading Bands" and would gather in the back room of the After Dark nightclub to pretend to be their friends and try to capture some of their magic.

This is still pretty much the strategy that you will see being advised on local music message boards up and down the country: play in your home town until you have built up a following and wait for the world to come to you. Don't believe a word of it. The professional music industry may be full of sharks, cheats and chancers, but believe me it is more of a meritocracy than your local music scene will ever be. In an ideal world the cream would rise to the top, but it is usually a song-less folk-rock band with quirky waistcoats or a pub rock band who have honed their impression of their heroes to perfection. There is also the fairly obvious question of why having an abnormally large number of personal acquaintances (which is usually what it takes to headline your local equivalent of Bar Oz) should be considered the acid test. If you can't tell already, I was extremely bad at this approach and could barely get my (admittedly poor) band a gig.

Instead, when I launched Mr Fogg in 2005 I decided to do what my idea of a "real" band would do: release a single and go on tour. I got 500 CDs made, recruited a bassist and keyboard player without hearing them play and headed off around the UK for a week in an extremely unreliable Vauxhall Astra. Around the same time, Myspace was in the process of affecting a generational shift in the way music was promoted. Myspace may be considered something of a joke now, but in my view its impact on music was far greater than that of Twitter or Facebook. Even now nothing has quite captured the magic of the early days of Myspace. In fact if you put together a Facebook page, a Twitter account and a Soundcloud stream it pretty much adds up to the original Myspace profile.

The thing that blew my mind about Myspace was that you could reach people from all over the world with just a click of a button. I remember uploading my first two songs late one night and the next morning waking up to find comments from New York, Montreal and Paris from people saying how much they liked them. I hadn't even had to leave my room. In the early days the community only really consisted of musicians, and I ended up discovering and chatting with a whole series of interesting people. One day I received a message that sent my mind spinning from a girl in Germany who told me she was planning on getting one of my song titles tattooed across her shoulder. I suggested she should think carefully before doing something so drastic, but she went ahead and sent me a photo a few days later. The idea that somebody from a country that I had never even visited could discover my music and become that level of fan was amazing to me. It certainly made the idea of fortnightly shows at Bar Oz less appealing.

****

By the time my first album was finished I realised that as many people were listening to my music on Myspace from abroad as from the UK and I cooked up a madcap idea to take advantage. I sent a message out asking people to recommend a venue in their local town where I should play. One of the first responses was from a teenager in Vilnius, Lithuania, so off I went.

When I arrived in Vilnius, accompanied by a trombonist, keyboard player and drummer, I found a freezing cold, empty city (it was November) with the occasional fur-hatted woman popping in and out of the boutiques in the city centre. The venue itself was a collective-run space underneath an office block, and the show was fairly unremarkable except for some memorably unpleasant pizza and the fact that everybody seemed to take great pleasure in verbally abusing the sound engineer's assistant, not least the engineer himself.

Unlike in the UK, it's normal for promoters on the continent to provide food and accommodation for bands and on this occasion the promoter in question had organized for us to stay in what he described as a "hostel". I was extremely grateful, because the cost of putting four people up in a hotel would have made it difficult to justify the trip – and a hostel sounded perfectly fine. He offered to drive us to our digs and said the engineer's assistant would show us where everything was.

We left the venue pretty late and it was between two and three a.m. when we pulled into a development of old Soviet apartment blocks. I knew immediately that something wasn't quite right but couldn't put my finger on it. Andy, the keyboard player, said his parents used to live in a similar looking building in Russia and that once inside the apartments were often quite nice. But then I realised what was wrong: everything was pitch black. It may have been three in the morning, but you could tell immediately that large sections of the development were uninhabited.

The door of our building was unlocked, and we found ourselves in a barely perceptible orange glow at the bottom of a flight of stairs. Andy said afterwards that he knew immediately that something was wrong because a cat relieved itself in the corridor in front of him and cats hate being dirty. If that sounds to you like the kind of thing somebody might say to you just before you wake up from a particularly weird dream then you are on the right track.

As always, I was carrying far too much equipment and it took me an age to drag all the gear up four or five flights of stairs. The others kept getting ahead, and every time I fell behind in the darkness I could feel panic rising in the pit of my stomach at the thought of what else might be going on in that building. It was like being in one of those horror movies where the characters insist on going into what look like the most obviously dangerous places and you can't believe they haven't turned back.

We eventually reached the top of the building and entered a corridor where the orange was ever so slightly brighter. Whereas before we had been stumbling blindly in the darkness, now we could see exactly what we had got ourselves into. In the gloom we could see that the edges of the corridor were crawling with rats that were in turn dodging used needles and assorted rubbish. Every now and again we would pass an inhabited apartment with a military-looking security system and a steel-reinforced door. Obviously some people still lived here, but I couldn't work out whether they were people we should be sympathetic towards or terrified of.

With a short-lived feeling of relief, I followed the band into a brightly lit doorway at the end of the corridor. I was expecting the doorway to lead into an apartment. Instead, I found three musicians and the engineer's assistant crammed into a single, tiny room. Inside was a desk with a 1980s computer and a copy of Russian Playboy, a camping gas stove with the remains of a week-old meal and a revolting couch that looked like it had survived a long history of abuse. Just as I was getting my bearings and trying to calculate whether there was even enough floor-space to accommodate all of us, our guide asked us whether we were likely to want to visit the bathroom during the night.

I don't know about you, but I have always thought it kind of normal to use the bathroom when I'm staying somewhere overnight. If the question itself wasn't ominous enough, the uncertainty in his voice certainly was. So we trooped back out into the corridor. The first thing I saw when I walked into the bathroom was sewage seeping through the floor in the middle of the room. On one wall was some angry looking graffiti and on the other a bank of grubby wash basins. At the end were two long-drop toilets with stains all the way up the walls. It's difficult to describe just how disgusting and unsettling the whole thing was. The stench was horrific.

Guillaume, the drummer, had sensibly declined the bathroom tour, and we returned to the first room to find him getting some well-soiled sleeping bags out of a cupboard in the corner. It was obvious that thirty years of passers-through had made use of those sleeping bags since they had last been washed, but Guillaume – without the benefit of having seen the plumbing facilities – seemed willing to give it a go. The whole experience had been overwhelming, and I was so exhausted by this point that my brain seemed to be working at half speed. But as the situation escalated I realised that there was no way we could stay there. Perhaps on another occasion I would have gritted my teeth, closed my eyes and waited until morning, but I knew that I couldn't put the others through it. I vividly remember feeling a great weight of responsibility for our 22-year old trombonist Faye and knowing that there was no way she could spend the night in that place. With hindsight we should have turned back as soon as we entered the building, but somehow in the middle of it all everything seemed less extraordinary.

Having made my mind up, I began to think about how we could get out of there. I was sensitive to the fact that we were guests in this place and that our hosts obviously felt that it was an appropriate place for us to stay. I thanked our guide for showing us everything and said that we could take it from there. A puzzled look crossed his face. It was only then that I realised that he was planning on staying there with us. Even just in terms of square feet there was no way we could all have slept in there at the same time. In the end I had to tell him straight that there was no way we could sleep there. I woke up my parents in the UK and asked them to Google the first mainstream international brand of hotel that they could find in Vilnius. I offered to take our guide with us, but he said he was happy to stay. I felt extremely sorry for him: he clearly felt guilty for bringing us somewhere that we were uncomfortable with and I didn't like the idea of him staying there alone – or that he might not have a choice.

We tried four different taxi companies before any was willing to come and pick us up – it was obviously a part of town that you didn't go to in the early hours of the morning. When we did eventually manage to persuade somebody to come, Andy went out to the road and tried manically to wave down any car in sight (of which there were very few). The night ended when we arrived at the Novotel in the city centre just as the police were being called to break up a bloody fight that was taking place between two drunks in the lobby. Looking back, the whole thing seems scarcely believable.

The following day we travelled to Latvia to play in Riga, which was even colder than Vilnius. We played in a very nice club by the river where I think I played my first ever encore. It was such an unexpected request that we were backstage for several minutes before we realised that the cheering was for us to come back on. The accommodation was – thankfully – the flat of one of the venue staff. We slept on cushions on the floor but couldn't have been more grateful after the previous night's drama. That went for me at least. When Faye dropped out of playing for Mr Fogg a month or two later one of the reasons she gave was that she had been forced to stay in a what she called a co-ed "squat" in Riga. I was disappointed at the time that she seemed oblivious to the pressure I had been under the night before to find somewhere safe for us to stay, but you can hardly blame her. She signed up to play trombone, not sleep on a stranger's floor in a foreign country, even if it was a floor in a nice flat and not remotely a squat.

You might think that this experience would make me think twice about conducting similar experiments, but the more I play abroad the harder

I find it to stomach the aggressive trendiness of the UK music scene or the exceptional smugness of some of the people who work in it. Yes, London is a great music city whose influence extends all over the world, but its patronising attitude towards less zeitgeisty places is unwarranted. As a result I've played shows in Iceland, Slovenia, Poland, Germany, Belgium, France, Italy, the US and many other countries, staying in people's houses, rooms above music venues and even a military barracks that had been taken over by a creative collective in Ljubljana.

Even disregarding how much more open-minded and decentralised music scenes are outside of the UK, for anybody making niche or non-chart music the UK simply isn't big enough to sustain you on its own. If you can build a cult following in several different countries, however, it soon adds up to a substantial audience. Fortunately, the advent of Facebook, Twitter and Youtube means that the digital borders between countries are increasingly fluid. And if you can't find a rational reason to go and play outside of your city, state or country, do it for the amazing experiences you'll have and the people you'll meet.

In the summer of 2012 I travelled to Messina on the Italian island of Sicily to play a small festival. It was a typically complicated Mr Fogg weekend: show in London on Friday; festival in Italy on Saturday; wedding in Hertfordshire on Sunday. The plan was that I would drive straight from the show in London to the airport, leave my suit in the van ready for the wedding and then rent another vehicle in Sicily. After the festival I would simply fly back, pick up the van and drive to the wedding.

To start with, everything went to plan. The only snag was being pulled over by the police at 3am on the way to the airport and having a typically passive-aggressive conversation with two officers at the side of the road. If you drive around a lot in the middle of the night, you get used to these exchanges. On this occasion they wanted to test me for drink driving, but their breathalyser was broken. They conceded that there was in any case nothing to indicate that I had been drinking, but then tried to suggest that it was clear from my eyes that I had been taking drugs. As it happens I don't drink, don't smoke and don't take drugs. I don't even drink tea or coffee. I really am one of those squares who are genuinely in it only for the music. The only downside is that it does give me a propensity to be somewhat sarcastic towards police officers who pull me over in the middle of the night. I suggested that they should either produce some evidence or sling their hook. They acquiesced, and I continued to the airport for my scheduled three hours' sleep before my flight the next day.

Once in Sicily, I rented a car at Palermo airport and drove to Messina for the show. I remember really enjoying the performance, which was right on the beach. It was mainly attended by local teenagers: blinking boys with slicked back hair linking arms with apparently contented trophy girlfriends dressed up to the nines. It all seemed very old-fashioned to me, but they liked the music.

As usual the promoter had arranged for somewhere for me to stay (a hotel, thankfully), but he hadn't given me the details and was nowhere to be seen in the heaving crowd when I was ready to leave. After a series of unsuccessful enquiries, a total stranger eventually handed me a note saying that a room was booked for me in the name of

Micelli at the Royal Hotel, which was at either 23 or 123 Cannizaro - he couldn't remember which.

I drove to 23 Cannizaro; there was no Royal Hotel. I drove to 123 Cannizaro; there was no Royal Hotel. I phoned my contact at the festival; there was no answer. In the end I found a hotel called the Royal Palace Hotel, which was at number 3 Cannizaro. It had to be it. I parked my car by the railway station and proceeded to lug my suitcase to the hotel. Little did I know, the only people who park their cars by the station in Messina at 3am are curb-crawlers and as soon as I stepped out of the car I was met by a series of whistles and catcalls.

Having dodged the crowd of women, I rang the night bell at the Royal Palace Hotel. A very stiff looking man said that there was no booking in the name of Micelli and that in any case it was very unlikely they would have booked that hotel for me; they would probably have chosen something cheaper. Back on the street, I returned to my car for the note, to see whether he might be persuaded by documentary evidence of the booking (even if it did have the name of the wrong hotel and the wrong address). On the way back the catcalls began again. I felt like I was in a Kafkaesque nightmare – at 3am, dripping with sweat in the searing heat and surrounded by a surreal crowd of cackling prostitutes. When I got back to the car, I looked up from fumbling with my keys to see one of the girls open the passenger door and try to climb in.

Back at the Royal Palace, the stiff man was unimpressed by my sheet of paper. He said there was another hotel with a similar name that I should try up the road. I tried three. None of them had a reservation in the name Micelli. Eventually, after an hour of dragging my case around the streets of Messina and three visits to the Royal Palace Hotel, I checked into a grotty but cheap place around the corner.

I set my alarm for 5:30am to give me enough time to drive back to Palermo to catch my plane, but slept through until gone six. I still had time – I had been cautious with my alarm setting – but I would now have to put my foot down to get there in time. I returned to the car and put my key in the ignition. Nothing happened. I tried again. Nothing. Knowing that I was probably fifteen minutes away from missing my plane I phoned the hire company, but the office was shut. I tried to phone the breakdown number instead, but they just offered to send a truck in an hour's time. I was sure there must be some way they could help over the phone, but nobody was available. I consulted the manual; I even tried ringing the car's manufacturer in the UK, but nobody would answer. Eventually, having lost valuable time and sure to miss the flight, I got through to somebody at the AA in the UK who said it was the immobiliser and all I had to do was jiggle the steering wheel in a particular way and the car would start as normal. It was annoying enough to miss the flight – and the wedding – but even more so knowing that I could have made it if I'd just been a bit luckier - or a bit less brainless.

At the airport I spent a long time arguing with the hire company (I had plenty of time after all – there was no flight until the next day), but they refused to accept any liability, despite my protestations that their helpline had failed to answer my questions. I was resigned to defeat and humiliation but in any case asked for details of the complaints procedure. While I was waiting for the agent to come back with the details, one of his colleagues in a Fiat 500 took a high-speed shortcut through a neighbouring parking space and ran over my bag, damaging both my laptops.

If I was superstitious I might be tempted to see this trip as a message to give up touring. Instead, you should see it as a positive. I have already used up all the bad luck, so go ahead: knock yourself out.

D.I.Y

The music industry is like an onion, with the epicentre surrounded by layers of gatekeepers who each speak their own particular flavour of jargon. From the outside it seems impenetrable: you need an agent to get you gigs, a PR team to get you in the press, a plugger to get you on the radio or TV, a distributor to get your records in the shops, a label to manage the campaign and a manager to keep everybody on track. The list goes on.

For artists starting out it can feel like there is a hidden, inaccessible world deep within the layers of the onion in which sophisticated experts perform highly complex work out of public view. That is exactly the impression that these people want you to have. The language they speak – label copy, plots, impact dates, targets – is designed to keep as many people on the outside as possible. I have seen inside and I can let you in on a secret:

even in the darkest, most closely guarded parts of the onion all anybody is doing is sending emails.

Consider the agent. His job is to email people to find out whether they would like to book you for a concert. The radio plugger emails people and asks whether they would like to play your song on the radio. The PR agency emails journalists and asks whether they would like to write an article about you. The manager emails the record label to persuade them to get everybody else to send as many emails as possible. That's it. That's what the inhabitants of the onion spend 90-95% of their time doing.

When Barter Jr. used to give me reports on meetings I had attended myself on the peculiar premise that I wouldn't have understood what was going on, he was doing it to justify his particular role in the music industry dance. The rest of them are doing exactly the same thing. In the intervening years I have held dozens of similar meetings without a manager and have never yet had to call in a translator.

Now, I am not for a moment saying that there isn't a place for expertise, nor that the relationships that an agent builds with promoters or that a plugger builds with radio producers over the years are not valuable. But the more you educate yourself about where the value is really being created, the better position you will be in to spend your limited resources wisely. And in the event that all the services of the various types of gatekeepers are out of your reach, remember that the ability to create new contacts is far more valuable than an existing network. These people are just sending emails, and so can you.

The other 5% of the music industry is the genuinely complicated part: ISRC codes, PPL, MCPS, PRS, producer points, publishing agreements and all the rest of it. This is the 5% that made the music industry so slow to adapt to technological change; the licensing implications of new digital business models are enough to give anybody a serious headache. This 5% is harder to get to grips with, but it can be done, and it may be worth it, because these are the things that determine whether and how much you get paid.

Most of us would like to spend all our time making music and let somebody else worry about the nitty-gritty. There are two main reasons why you should give the boring stuff at least some of your attention: first, because if you hire every available expert you will need to be exceptionally successful to make any kind of living and, just as importantly, if you don't understand what's going on, you won't be able tell whether people are doing a good job on your behalf.

My first forays into the world of DIY were not the result of any great strategic thinking; it just seemed like the obvious thing to do. When I finished my first Mr Fogg recordings, I decided that I wanted to release a single. I found somebody to design the artwork, got the CDs manufactured and wrote to all the independent record shops in the UK asking if they would be willing to take a handful. To my surprise several of them said yes, and I sent bundles of five or ten CDs each to the likes of Piccadilly Records and On The Fringe - sadly, there are not many of those kinds of shops left these days. I also wrote a press release and sent the music off to every blog, magazine or radio station I could find an address for. At this stage, I had barely even told any of my friends about Mr Fogg, because I thought there was a reasonable chance the music was rubbish, but favourable reviews starting coming in from fanzines and then eventually larger publications like Drowned In Sound and Hot Press. I re-wrote the press release to include all of this, made up a new release date two months later and sent it off again to all the people who hadn't responded the first time around.

One morning I was in my parents' kitchen when the phone rang. It was a sheer coincidence that I picked up the phone because nobody ever called there for me, but instead of a message for one of my parents it was Louise Kattenhorn from Radio 1 asking to speak to Mr Fogg. She told me that Rob Da Bank had picked out my song *Giving In* from the demo pile and was going to play it that night. Would I be willing to phone back and leave an answerphone message to be broadcast on the show? Since then I have been played on the radio many times and there is always something magical about listening to your song along with a million other people, but that was without doubt one of the most exciting days of my life.

I re-wrote the press release a second time and managed to persuade John Kennedy at XFM and Tom Robinson at 6Music to play it too. Tom even made it his record of the week – a little song that I had made myself in the spare bedroom with a £30 microphone.

Around the same time I spent three months working as an intern at One Little Indian Records, home to Björk, one of my favourite artists. I learned a huge amount there by going out to shows every night and listening to the founder Derek Birkett's stories at the bar, but the biggest lesson I learned was that they didn't have a magic key or secret password any more than I did. Derek had started the label as an outlet for the records he was producing in the eighties and early nineties, and it had somehow morphed into one of the country's biggest independent record companies. They were doing what I was doing, just on a much bigger scale.

Despite this realisation it was still incredibly flattering when the labels came calling, and over the next couple of years I released a string of singles on different labels, culminating in the collaboration with EMI for *Stung*. But when I had grown tired of the slog of A&R meetings and artistic compromise I decided to release my own album rather than wait for somebody to do it for me.

At first, I followed all the rules of the mainstream music industry, hiring an unsustainable team of every kind of PR person, from national radio to regional press to student and club promotion, all overseen by a marketing consultant. I even had a top ten "hit" in the UK club chart with a remix of *Moving Parts* that sounded nothing like the original.

The marketing consultant was the first to go. After a couple of weeks I realised that all he was doing was forwarding emails from me to other members of the team while charging me a small fortune. Everybody else did a professional job by and large, but I would have had to sell an enormous quantity of records to make the money back.

I also began to realise that the rights of access that they had to the media were not exclusive. The radio plugger told me that Janice Long – a Radio 2 DJ who had been a big supporter of my music – was not interested in playing anything from the album. I bumped into her in a coffee shop shortly afterwards and it was clear that she hadn't even heard it. Probably the plugger had sent an email to her producer and received no reply and that was the end of that. Janice asked for a CD, played it on Radio 2 a few days later and invited me in for a live session. Later she asked for me to send music directly to her home address. A different plugger told me a similar story about Tom Robinson, so I turned up at a conference he was speaking at so that I could just happen to bump into him. He also was unaware that a new Mr Fogg album even existed and played a song from it on the radio two weeks afterwards. As a musician himself, I suspect he is no more a fan of arbitrary barriers to entry than I am. Since then, I have always sent him my music directly.

The positive results of this DIY approach go on and on: securing articles about Poirier's remix of *Keep Your Teeth Sharp* simply by researching which bloggers were fans of his music and writing to them myself; putting myself forward to live-tweet for Guardian Music from Reading Festival; going to a gig by an XFM DJ's favourite artist and talking to them at the bar; encountering Jo Whiley in a café and her later saying on Radio 2 that she had eaten egg and chips with Mr Fogg and he seemed like a very nice chap. A lot of this reflects the randomness of working in music, but it also goes to show that doing things the "right away" or going through "appropriate channels" is not the be-all and end-all.

You will, though, have to be committed to the possibilities of DIY not to be put off by the professionals. They will take the credit or claim exceptional circumstances and will almost certainly take offence, because becoming redundant is their greatest fear. One of the most depressing of all my encounters with music industry gate keepers was a phone call with a short-lived manager of mine called Patrick Spinks. I had sent him an email following up on some pitches he had agreed to make. He didn't reply, so I telephoned a couple of days later. I asked him whether he had received the email. "I did. But, Phil, this is the way this works. If I have any news, *I* will call *you*. Good bye." He put the phone down. It is so tempting to put this kind of patronising behaviour down to "professionalism" or "how things are done". Don't stand for it.

****

The jargon-based defence may be particularly bad in music, but it extends to almost any industry you can name. Filmmaking is no exception. Following the successful debut of the marching band at Reading Festival in 2010, I set out on a music video project that put my onion-peeling skills to the sternest of tests. The concept for the video was a single shot performance that started off looking like it was in a small studio, but then turned out to be in the middle of Trafalgar Square in London. The effect would be achieved by putting a camera with a very powerful zoom on top of a nearby building, with the square gradually being taken over by Mr Fogg imagery, culminating in a marching band.

The usual approach for a project like this is to hire a producer to oversee the project. He or she will then put together the team to deliver the video. I duly approached several producers whose cost estimates ranged between £25,000 and £50,000. When I asked what exactly would cost so much they gave responses like "It's a fifty grand idea" or "It's not going to be cheap to film in Trafalgar Square". I had nowhere near £50,000 to spend on a music video, but I wasn't convinced by the vague responses. I decided to do my own research.

The first port of call was the Greater London Authority, which is responsible for Trafalgar Square. If I couldn't get permission, the idea was a non-starter. Much to my surprise, there was a set process for applying to film in the square and the charge was just £500 an hour. I would only be able to afford one hour, but making a music video in an hour wasn't beyond the realms of possibility. The application form itself, however, consisted of seventeen pages of terms, conditions and local bylaws. For a programme designed to widen access to public spaces, it was certainly a pretty intimidating document. But, after I had waded through the pages of terminology and jargon, I realised that all it really amounted to was taking out insurance, using no built structures and taking care not to injure members of the public.

The next part of the process was to organise the shoot itself. People kept telling me that I needed somebody on the team with experience of a similarly large project, but I couldn't work out what they would actually *do*. Instead, I brought on board two young filmmakers called Ed and Stuart who couldn't quite believe my idea was serious but were willing to see if it could be done. Among other things I became an expert on film cameras and lenses, bought radio licenses and ordered giant balloons and a canister of helium to be delivered to my flat. Once I thought we had everything lined up and ready to go, I sent my budget to one of the producers who thought it couldn't be done and asked what we were missing. The reply came back: "Walkie talkies?"

It was obvious to me by then that the reason nobody thought it was possible to shoot a video in Trafalgar Square for less than £25,000 was because they couldn't see through the layers of the onion – all the things that you "have" to do if you're going to make a "professional" music video, like hire a first assistant director, have an art department or buy in expensive catering. We got to the same endpoint by breaking everything down into a series of small tasks: order ten umbrellas; phone five military bands; seek permission from the National Gallery to put a camera on the roof; cast a model for the Mr Fogg sandwich board; order spray paint. It was a lot of work, but it definitely wasn't rocket science. The day before the shoot my manager phoned me up to tell me that he had spoken to his cousin, who was a stage designer, and he had told him that it wasn't possible to spray an MF logo onto a white umbrella because of the domed shape. If that doesn't give you an indication of how straitjacketed the minds of experts can be I'm not sure what will.

A key part of the video was of course the marching band. For the Reading Festival performance I had put together my own, but for this video I wanted something much bigger, so I ended up recruiting a youth drum and bugle corps from Surrey. The band rehearsed on Wednesday nights and the video shoot was on the following Thursday, so as it turned out the only time that I would be able to see them play was the night before filming. It was only then I realised that they couldn't actually play the song.

The rehearsal took place in a fenced-off corner of a military firing range, miles away from anywhere. I spent the first hour with the percussionists, who had been struggling with the snare drum rhythms. When I went into the main hall to hear what the brass sounded like, I was greeted by chaos. One of the most memorable moments was when the bandleader came up to me and asked whether they should pay attention to the sharp symbols on the score. "Well it *is* a different note", I replied. I asked him if he had played the recording of the song to the band. "Not yet". It then turned out that nobody in the room could actually remember the fingering for the note in question. Eventually I heard it coming from a corner of the room and was very grateful to learn that one of the youngest members of the troupe, a euphonium player, had worked it out.

I later realised that I had broken the band's system. They were using instruments from the US school band model, which are all tuned to the key of G and all use the same fingering, the idea being that any child can play any instrument. All the music is written in the treble clef, but the instruments sound at different octaves. It is an extremely clever idea, which allows high schools to tackle complex music with amateur musicians. Unfortunately, I had put the cat among the pigeons by asking them to play in a key that wasn't G major or E minor. We got there though - it ended with me conducting the rehearsal, shouting cues over the din, while the parents filed in to pick up their kids.

While the band packed away their equipment, I retreated to my car, where I telephoned my future-wife Jo to tell her that I was in deep trouble and that there was at least some chance that the marching band would prove to be a total disaster. As I ended the call, I realised that everything had gone dark. They had all gone home. I started the car and headed out of the military compound where the rehearsal had taken place, but the gate was locked. I ended up caged in a yard surrounded by ten-foot barbed wire fences for almost an hour before I could get hold of anybody to let me out. For a while it felt like there was an outside possibility that I would still be there the following morning, instead of making a music video in Trafalgar Square.

When I walked into Trafalgar Square on the day itself, I was struck by just how enormous it was. The idea of making a music video there seemed almost absurd. Even now, I have the same feeling every time I walk through or drive past. It just didn't – and still doesn't – seem possible that it could actually be done. As we only had permission to film for one hour, everything had to be meticulously planned in advance, so we did walk-through after walk-through before our allotted time - which nearly got us thrown out of the square.

When you're shooting a music video, usually the performance is recorded in sync to the track and then the music – *Answerphone* in this case - is overlaid afterwards. It means that it doesn't have to sound good on the day, but it does have to be perfectly synchronised in order to look convincing. Because in this case fifty people, including a troupe of dancers and the camera operators, all had to be in sync, I had created a version of the song with a metronome running all the way through. There would be no editing afterwards, so everybody's movements were locked in to cues matched to particular beats of the song.

Most important of all for the final video was that the marching band was in sync. I calculated the exact number of steps that it would take them to walk across the square and matched that to cues in the music. The only problem was getting them to stay in time. There was no way I was going to be able to provide earpieces for every single member of the band, so I gave the ones I did have to the drummers. The rest of the band should be playing to the percussion section, so in theory they were the only people that needed to be able to hear the recording.

I conducted a series of run-throughs with the drummers, telling them that it was absolutely essential that they count in as loudly as possible so that everybody started at the same time.

I showed them how it was done: "One! Two! Three! Four!!!"

They had a go: "…".

I tried it again, louder: "ONE! TWO! THREE! FOUR!!!"

Then it was their turn: "…"

I realised that they were either too shy or too terrified to open their mouths, smiled and told them it would be all right on the night. I then set about desperately trying to get hold of Guillaume, Mr Fogg's drummer. On the roof of the National Gallery, the technical team were having a similarly calm conversation with the hire company, who had sent us a faulty zoom lens. The replacement arrived less than half an hour before our agreed one-hour slot.

An hour of filming gave us enough time to complete four takes of the performance. For the first two, the drummers did exactly the same as they had in rehearsal, and the band made their entrance at the wrong time and in a wide-eyed panic. Then, to my relief, Guillaume turned up and took over one of the earpieces. If you watch the finished video closely, you can see him walking alongside them with a pair of drum sticks, screaming out the count. Without that, we might never have got a useable take.

Everything else went better than I could ever have imagined. I had hired a small handful of extras to play the part of interested members of the public, but they were swallowed up by a mass of several hundred tourists who formed a gauntlet running down the steps of the square as though it had been scripted. It sounded frankly terrible on the day – me singing unamplified without any kind of backing, and the band playing the same notes over and over again – but the atmosphere was amazing. Standing there alone in the middle of Trafalgar Square at the start of each take, knowing what was about to unfold, felt like the most dangerous but also the most exciting thing I'd ever done. I spent a long time afterwards having my photo taken with members of the crowd who assumed I must be important: "Can I have a photo with you, please? And who are you anyway?"

The footage shot from the top of the National Gallery was incredible, and I have to admit I took great pleasure in sending it to all the experts who had said it couldn't be done. Since then, I've only become more sceptical of people telling me that my ideas are unrealistic or that I need a team of specialists to pull it off. Sometimes they are right, but more often than not you can prove them wrong by breaking down the challenge into the simplest possible parts. Any big task is just a series of smaller tasks piled on top of each other. Break it down yourself and it's easy to see which ones require specialist expertise and which just a bit of elbow grease. Artists have an advantage over the experts in breaking down complexity, because the core requirement is something that comes naturally to us – imagination.

There's More To Life

"I'll take the first flight home - Try to hold on"

On the 26th of May 2012 I was in Utrecht on tour to promote my second album, *Eleven,* which was due to be released a couple of weeks later. I was in the middle of a run of European dates that had already taken in Italy, Germany and Poland and was in Utrecht to play a roof party run by a local collective before heading on to Amsterdam, Copenhagen, Berlin and Rome. For this particular leg of the tour I was travelling alone to save costs.

It was oppressively hot in the city, and I was scheduled to play in the full glare of the sun on the roof of an apartment block. There was nowhere to hide, and, as I waited to play I sought some relief by staying as close to the walls of the building as possible, trying to find an inch or two of shade. As time wore on, an eclectic bunch of friends and friends of friends of the collective drifted up onto the roof to enjoy the sunshine and to hear the trippy, improvised techno being played by the support band. One of the great thrills of travelling and playing music is to experience these kinds of situations and I was enjoying the buzz of thinking self-indulgently about what some of my more straight-laced friends and family might make of the scene.

I spoke to an Englishman with a faux-American accent who had been on a lifelong search for the ultimate libertarian state. Most recently he had been living in Scandinavia, but had moved to the Netherlands for the music and the freedom to smoke as much marijuana as he pleased. He spoke – in sentences that ended only with the word "man" – about his philosophy of life and his admiration for the laid-back scene in Utrecht. But when I asked him what he did for a living, the veneer cracked: "IT, man".

The rest of the crowd were of a similar ilk. They had all either dropped out of the real world to pursue music, art or writing, or hadn't quite escaped the pressures of the rat race but still allowed themselves to live the dream at the weekends, especially in the hot summer months on rooftops like this one. We seemed to get on well, and the show was greeted with warm, spaced-out applause.

After the show I got talking to a very friendly man who had supplied the party with beer from his own microbrewery. I was listening to his explanation of the craft-brewing scene in Utrecht when I noticed that I had three missed calls from my mother.

I called her back. I could tell immediately from her voice that she was struggling to remain calm and that it had to be bad news. She told me that my father had fallen unconscious during a family meal to celebrate his 68th birthday and was being taken to hospital in an ambulance. She was getting into the ambulance now to travel with him and would phone again from the hospital.

By the time the phone went dead, the eccentric charms of the roof terrace had gone sour. A few minutes ago I had been in the middle of another exciting adventure; now I was stuck on a rooftop in a foreign country with a group of total strangers who were operating under a fug of alcohol and weed. I felt a deep feeling of detachment from both the catastrophe that was unfolding back home and from the jokes, stories and polemics of the crowd on the rooftop. I didn't know how to tell them what had happened, so instead I nodded and smiled weakly as they talked - and waited for the phone to ring.

The more time passed without news, the more serious I knew the situation must be; they would have told me if he had woken up. I could feel the tension in my stomach making it hard to breathe. I phoned back an hour later and was told that my father had entered a deeper level of coma. A scan of his brain was being sent to specialists in Southampton.

Everything seemed to escalate so rapidly. I was told to make arrangements to return to the UK. Then, in the next phone call, my sister told me that my father had suffered a massive bleed to his brain and that there was nothing the doctors could do to save him.

People describe things as unbelievable all the time. But this genuinely felt like it couldn't be real. Three hours earlier my dad had been enjoying his birthday party; now he was fighting for his life. I remember vividly the pavement in the car park below the apartment block where I sat down to tell Jo the news, with the sounds of the roof party still wafting down from above. In my memory, though,

I'm standing in the road, watching myself make the phone call.

I wandered around the building in a state of shock for several minutes and then slowly began to collect my equipment together. I felt like I was moving in a different dimension to the partygoers, who were still drinking and laughing merrily. Eventually one of them asked me if everything was OK – he had seen me talking on the phone. When I told him that my father was going to die, he was so shocked that he burst into tears.

Once they knew what was happening, everybody was fantastic. Between them they carried all my gear down the stairs and loaded the van, before sending me on my way to the airport. I put *In Rainbows* on the CD player and sang to myself all the way there. The first available ticket was in KLM business class at six o'clock the following morning so I spent the night asleep on the floor in the airport. I took a photo of my distorted, exhausted face so that I would be able to remember what it felt like afterwards. As I made my way into the plane's half-empty business class section with sunglasses covering my swollen eyes, I couldn't resist a very brief gallows chuckle at the thought that somebody might put the expensive plane ticket and the outfit together and think that they were travelling with a pretentious rock star, rather than just a nobody living through a crisis.

My father passed away thirty six hours later, having been in a coma for nearly three days. After what seemed like weeks in limbo in the hospital, sleeping on the floor by my father's bed, leaving almost gave an illusion of relief. But what I had never really appreciated before it happened to me was that major events like the death of a family member don't just impact on the present; they distort the future too. There would always be somebody missing in our family from now on. Getting over his death wasn't so much a case of dealing with the shock and grief as getting used to him not being there. He doesn't know that I got into Oxford University; he doesn't know that Jo and I are married; he doesn't know that he has a baby granddaughter.

It seems of little consequence now, but that week should have been one of the most exciting and important of my musical career. I was in the middle of a tour that I had spent six months organising and was about to release my second album, which had been a year in the making. Some of my family said that I should finish the tour, which would be over by the time of the funeral, but there was no way I could leave them behind to deal with everything. Instead I cancelled all my Mr Fogg commitments, and the album release came and went in the background with me barely noticing. It's maybe one of the biggest disadvantages of doing everything yourself that when you are unable to do it nobody else is there to pick up the file. In any case, most of the work of the previous year amounted to nothing.

My father had been a big influence on Mr Fogg. I would speak to him several times a week to ask his advice. When I first started out he thought it was idiotic to pursue such a financially precarious career (he was probably right), but when he realised that other people were taking my music seriously, he became my most fervent supporter. His death - and the anti-climax of *Eleven*'s release - felt like a full stop.

****

Two years later, having barely performed in the intervening period and in the middle of my course at Oxford, I received an invitation to play a festival in Utrecht, organised by the same collective who had organised the roof party. There was no real justification for travelling all that way with no record to promote - the fee would cover the travel costs, but not much more - but for two years the image of that roof and the car park below had been indelibly printed on my brain. The suffocating heat, the people and the events of that day seemed like the plot of a movie more than real life. I had to go back to see for myself that they were real.

So it was that in July 2014 I returned to Utrecht. The festival was taking place not on the roof terrace but in a series of clubs around the city. I had arranged to perform with two cellists and briefly felt the buzz of adventure again as we put together our performance from scratch and I felt the thrill of hearing the sounds in my head coming to life in the room. But the charm of the place and the people had not returned.

The care-free organisers had neglected to provide the bass guitar and lights that we needed, to scale up their group of friends of friends to fill out the capacity of the festival or to arrange enough accommodation for all the artists. One of the team

– the same man who had burst into tears on hearing about my father – very generously offered the use of his flat, but there ended up being twice as many people as anticipated. I slept on the floor with a heavy metal band from Germany; a female photographer winked at me and said that we should save space by sharing a bed. Five years earlier, I might have delighted in re-telling anecdotes from this kind of trip. Now, it had lost its appeal.

Before I left Utrecht I returned to the roof terrace and the car park I had thought so much about over the previous two years. It could have been any apartment block in any city. I don't know what I expected to find, but they were perfectly plain and boring, not the surreal places of my memory. As I turned to leave I realised they no longer had any hold over me.

Never Give Up

The members of the bands that I used to play and dream with in Reading a decade or more ago have long since dispersed to proper grown-up careers. None of the people that packed out Bar Oz, swanned around the After Dark or came back from Camden with stars in their eyes are still making music. Those of us that are still at it are the ones that were only ever in it for the thrill of writing and performing music. The reality is that being a full-time musician is not a sensible decision on any rational basis. You only keep going if it is an addiction.

When I was seven years old I taught myself *The Sloop John B* by The Beach Boys on a plastic toy guitar with three strings, secretly staying up far beyond my bedtime to get it right. Once I got my hands on a keyboard - and later a real guitar - I spent every spare minute of every day writing songs. By the time I was ten I was selling an album I had recorded on twelve-minute message cassettes to my friends at school. In one English class we had to write an essay about what we wanted to do when we grew up and how school would help; I wrote that I was going to be a pop star and school wasn't going to help in the slightest. For as long as I can remember, whenever I have had a spare minute I have sat at the piano and written songs. Even now, there is not a single piece of music written by anybody else that I could play all the way through. For me it has always been about song writing. But even as a child, music was not a pursuit without obstacles.

In junior school I auditioned for the choir every year for six years – every single year that I was at the school – without getting in. By the time I got to the sixth form I was the only child of my age who was still interested enough to audition, and they still didn't let me in. The school had a fantastic music teacher called Mrs Hoare who used to enthuse about my rough and ready compositions, but my piano teacher vetoed a performance of one of the pieces in a school concert because she didn't approve of the title – *Dawn Baby Rock*.

When I arrived at senior school I discovered that there was a pre-ordained group of music department darlings who had all been taking violin or trumpet exams since the age of four and that everything was set up to support them. I took every music class that I could, but was more interested in the experiments I was conducting on my four track tape recorder at home than the tedious composition tasks the teacher, Mr Millard, set us. He was apparently deaf to melody and graded everything according to how many inversions or suspensions you had worked into your harmony. The result was that the music department told my parents that I should not take A-level music due to my lack of composition ability and harmonic understanding. I had taken up the bassoon by this point in order to try and get into the orchestra. My teacher, Mrs Tugwell, realised that I had musical talent and put a good word in for me. It made no difference.

When the time came to submit our GCSE compositions, we had the option to include a third piece that could not negatively affect the grade but might earn bonus marks. I played Mr Millard two of the songs that I had recorded on my four-track. He was totally flabbergasted – "*You* did this?" - not only by the quality of the songs but by the fact that I had programmed the drums, played guitar, bass and keyboards on the recording and produced a vocal performance by a local girl from my village. He apparently couldn't believe that somebody who didn't put the requisite number of second inversions into a school composition could be capable of such a thing. They still wouldn't let me do A-level music, though. My only victory over the music department was in rising to first bassoon in the Thames Vale Youth Orchestra. The school's head of music was the conductor; he was so surprised by what my section was able to achieve that he gave us a special mention in the AGM.

I am not so wrapped up in my own art that I don't realise that if my childhood musical exploits had been mind-blowing somebody would have noticed sooner rather than later - even now I expect the worst every time I send a new song out into the world. I would have got into the choir if my voice had been sufficiently angelic and probably without six auditions. What's curious is how by sheer force of determination and practice I ended up as a professional singer, even if my voice is still not the most technically proficient. My own analysis is that I probably did have some talent worth recognising, but didn't display it in conventional ways. The other part of the story is the hard work, perseverance and pure enjoyment that turned whatever talent I did have into songs that can be played on the radio. I only wish I could have followed my own advice and been brilliant enough to go even further. The celebrated talents of the darlings have long since been turned to other disciplines with the notable exception of a professional violinist called John Howarth.

****

Before Mr Fogg I would occasionally audition for other people's bands, based on the idea that it might be easier to join something that was already up and running than to start from scratch. The most popular way to advertise for musicians in those days was through an extremely convoluted voicemail system that was linked to the classifieds in the back of NME. It was considered bad form to mention the name of the band, which was convenient because it allowed advertisers to appear more successful than they really were. But it also meant that when you left your thirty-second sound bite after the beep there was always an outside possibility that the person picking up the messages might be famous.

The first audition I attended through this process was for a band called The Hedon who had "industry interest" and a manager who had previously "had some hits". I had been in Cheshire visiting family and drove three hours to get to the audition, which took place in a rehearsal studio near Shoreditch.

When I walked into the room, none of the band so much as looked me in the eye, let alone said hello. I eventually worked out that I was meant to plug my guitar into the Marshall amp in the corner, which barely worked. I struck up the riff from the song I had been asked to learn in advance, but was interrupted by the drummer, who told me that the band hadn't had time to prepare it. At this point the singer answered his mobile phone and walked out. The band's manager, sitting on a sofa in the corner, suggested that we "just jam", so we worked our way through an idea I had been working on. This didn't last long, though, because the singer came back in and said we would have to hurry up because a mate of his - obviously the preferred candidate for the job - was on his way.

He launched into a stream of improvised gibberish and nodded at the rest of us to play along, which we did, chaotically, for two minutes. Then he stopped and took out his phone again, making it clear that I should leave.

I'm generally quite mild mannered but something about the sheer arrogance of the whole episode pushed me over the edge. I embarked on an uninterrupted two-minute rant about how rude they were and how ridiculous it was that they hadn't bothered to learn their own song, culminating in me telling them I wasn't interested in joining their band and walking out in a huff.

They just stood there in silence throughout - I may as well have been telling them that they had nice hair. In fairness to the manager, he was decent enough to phone me the following day and apologise. He told me that he had given the band a good telling off and that he had really liked my guitar playing. It perhaps would have made a better story if the band had turned out to be The Kaiser Chiefs or The Strokes, but they sank without trace.

On another occasion I agreed to meet a guy called Ben with stripy hair, who had published an advert with a studied list of influences including Joy Division and Blondie. He boasted that his band was one of two or three acts that the music industry was gearing up to push into the charts that year and that he expected to sign a deal with Parlophone later that week. Because of all of this he couldn't risk telling me the name of the band. He wanted to sack the guitarist but needed to have his successor in place before he told him the bad news, hence the secrecy. He was very keen to tell me that the band had changed its sound in order to keep up with fashion. A few months ago their dominant influence had been hip-hop, but that was no longer cool so they were having to go electro and it had set them back several months.

Even better than any of this, though, was the fact that musical ability apparently wasn't necessary. Ben told me that the live show basically consisted of pouting and twiddling a few knobs. All I would have to do was pass a test to prove that I was sufficiently photogenic. He took a photo of me on his mobile phone – it was quite swish to have a camera phone in those days - and sent it to his band mates and manager for approval. I must have somehow shown myself to be trustworthy - or perhaps I had passed the photo test - because just before we parted he finally revealed the name of the band, Veto Silver. He ceremoniously produced a badge with the name printed on it from his jacket pocket, like a magician or a game show host. I looked them up on Myspace when I got home, discovered that it was a kind of indie boy band - their press spiel described them as "The best cheek-boned trio since Aha" - and thought nothing more about it.

Veto Silver never did sign to Parlophone or break into the charts, but I bumped into Ben at the 2006 Reading Festival, where I was playing for the first time. He was wandering around drunk in the VIP area. If you've ever wondered what it's like to hang out in the VIP area at a festival, you're not missing out on anything; it's almost entirely PR people, competition winners and hangers-on. When he saw me he did his best to escape, but I outfoxed him by being unexpectedly friendly. He apologised profusely for not having been in touch after our meeting and nearly fell over when I told him I had just played the Carling stage. I asked him how Veto Silver was going. He gave a smile that had a veneer of well-practised smugness but hinted at a deep vacuum beneath. "Very well, thank you. Very well indeed." He obviously wasn't quite ready to give up his role as a human advertising hoarding.

Three years earlier I had auditioned for a band with a rather less starry-eyed view of the music business. The manager, Warren, had been made redundant by London Records and had invested his pay settlement in a singer-songwriter called Richard Archer, whose band had been dropped by the same label. The pair had seen how much money the majors wasted at first hand and thought they could take them on. Archer's previous band had been offered a tour with Coldplay but had to turn it down because the label had spent the budget on music videos that nobody ever watched.

The music itself seemed strangely out-dated to me, like a throwback to Brit-pop from the mid-nineties. Somehow the production, which bulked out the songs with cheap-sounding synth strings, didn't measure up. But I liked their attitude and turned up to the audition with an open mind.

Aside from Richard, the only other member of the band was a drummer called Steve, so Richard played bass and sang. We spent a couple of hours together working on two songs: one - called *Living For The Weekend* - that I had been asked to learn in advance, and a new idea of Richard's with a dub-reggae rhythm and lyrics about a cash machine. I felt that Richard and I were getting on OK and what we played – stripped back to a three piece without the dodgy record production - actually sounded pretty good. But Steve and I didn't really see eye to eye, and my Smashing Pumpkins t-shirt and swooshy delay pedal seemed wildly out of sync with the band's style and ambitions. I was impressed with them as people, but it was obvious that it wasn't a good musical fit for either of us.

I kept an ear out to see whether they were making any progress, but years passed and I heard nothing. I assumed that the project had fallen by the wayside like so many others. But then one day I was driving home from a band practice when *Living For The Weekend* came on the radio. In 2006, four years after we had played together, Richard's band Hard-Fi went to number one in the UK charts with their debut album *Stars of CCTV*, the first of three top ten albums. *Living For The Weekend* turned out to be a number fifteen hit. *Cash Machine* (same lyrics, different tune) reached number fourteen.

You can say what you like about Hard-Fi's music – and I frequently have – but theirs is the ultimate story of perseverance and just goes to show what hard work can achieve. Richard's first band Contempo was dropped without releasing a record; six years later he was number one in the charts.

****

After the events of May 2012, I thought that I probably wouldn't get to make another Mr Fogg album. With both *Moving Parts* and *Eleven* I approached the writing and recording process with the mind-set that each of them could be the last record I ever made. With *Eleven* I had even included a kind of goodbye to music in the song *Oh Pearl*. The way things turned out didn't exactly seem like a message to change my mind.

But, before I knew it, I found myself sitting at the piano again, creating little sketches of songs. At first it was just an escape from everything that had happened and something constructive to do with my emotional energy. But after a while I started to think that maybe I would finish five of the best songs and make a new EP. Then I had more than five songs I liked and I thought it could be a mini-album. By the summer of 2013 I had written 37 songs.

I felt that there was an album somewhere in those sketches, but I didn't have the stomach to go out and persuade somebody to finance the recordings. Instead, when the BBC World Service moved out of Bush House, I bought the contents of Studio 16 at auction, covered my costs by selling the parts I didn't need and decided to produce the record myself. I didn't have great confidence in my mixing ability so I made sure that everything I recorded sounded as good as possible in the room. I rented my local church and arranged most of the album for strings, brass, piano and church organ. I would just stick two microphones up in the church and put the results on the record exactly as it sounded there and then.

The best of those recordings became the third Mr Fogg album, which will be released later this year.

As always, I have no idea what people will make of it, but those hours spent recording myself alone in the church, or up to my neck in piles of string scores, were some of the most rewarding musical experiences I have had. And if you get to make the music you want, what more could you ask for?

Lyric References

Be Brilliant:
Keep Your Teeth Sharp (Moving Parts)

Work With The Best:
Moving Parts (Moving Parts)

Do/Don't Sign With A Major:
Stay Out Of The Sun (Eleven)

Go Global:
Sprint (Eleven)

D.I.Y:
I Will Let You Down (Moving Parts)

There's More To Life:
Utrecht (Youth)

Never Give Up:
Oh Pearl (Eleven)

Index

6Music, 15, 46, 80

A Second Look, 43

A&R, 46, 50, 51, 55, 81

Adrien Brody, 25, 31, 34

After Dark, 58, 104

Answerphone, 52, 91

Arcade Fire, 15, 56

Bar Oz, 58, 59, 61, 104

BitTorrent, 54, 55

Björk, 41, 47, 51, 81

Brian Cranstone, 25

Damon Albarn, 44

Derek Birkett, 81

Drowned In Sound, 80

Dublin Castle, 58

Eleven, 52, 95, 101, 115, 119

EMI, 46, 47, 48, 49, 81

Facebook, 26, 60, 69

Feist, 44

Frank Gehry, 29

Giving In, 80

Goldrush, 51

Hard-Fi, 114, 115

Harry Barter, 36, 46

Hot Press, 80

Howie B, 47, 48

iTunes, 55, 56

Jamelia, 47

Janice Long, 82

Jerry Lee Lewis, 41

Jo Whiley, 83

John Kennedy, 80

Kazaa, 55

Keane, 46, 51

Keep Your Teeth Sharp, 83, 119

Killa Kela, 39

Kylie Minogue, 47

Limewire, 55

Ljubljana, 69

London Records, 113

Lost Prophets, 15

Macklemore, 56

Martin Rushent, 35, 49

Messina, 70, 71, 72, 73

Morning Runner, 51

Moving Parts, 10, 24, 43, 82, 115, 119

My Luminaries, 51

Myspace, 47, 59, 60, 61

NME, 52

Oh Pearl, 115, 119

On The Fringe, 79

One Little Indian Records, 81

Oxford University, 100

Patrick Spinks, 84

Peer Music, 47

Picadilly Records, 79

Pure Reason Revolution, 51

Q Magazine, 52

Radio 1, 15, 52, 80

Radio 2, 46, 52, 82, 83

Radiohead, 51, 54, 55, 56

Reading Festival, 15, 16, 45, 52, 83, 85, 88

Richard Archer, 113

Riga, 68

Rob Da Bank, 80

Shirley Bassey, 41

Spotify, 55

Stay Out Of The Sun, 52, 119

Stung, 40, 81

The Beach Boys, 104

The Bull and Gate, 58

The Good Natured, 51

The Guardian, 52

The Sloop John B, 104

Thom Yorke, 54, 55

Tom Robinson, 80, 83

Tony Kaye, 25, 26, 30, 32

Trafalgar Square, 85, 86, 87, 90, 93

Twitter, 15, 60, 69

U2, 47

Utrecht, 95, 97, 102, 103, 119

Valgeir Sigurðsson, 41

Vilnius, 61, 67, 68

XFM, 80, 83

Youtube, 69

Zane Lowe, 52